FINGERPICKING
POPULAR HITS

Arrangements by Bill LaFleur

ISBN 978-1-4950-2954-7

HAL•LEONARD®
CORPORATION

7777 W. BLUEMOUND RD. P.O. BOX 13819 MILWAUKEE, WI 53213

Visit Hal Leonard Online at
www.halleonard.com

INTRODUCTION TO FINGERSTYLE GUITAR

Fingerstyle (a.k.a. fingerpicking) is a guitar technique that means you literally pick the strings with your right-hand fingers and thumb. This contrasts with the conventional technique of strumming and playing single notes with a pick (a.k.a. flatpicking). For fingerpicking, you can use any type of guitar: acoustic steel-string, nylon-string classical, or electric.

THE RIGHT HAND

The most common right-hand position is shown here.

Use a high wrist; arch your palm as if you were holding a ping-pong ball. Keep the thumb outside and away from the fingers, and let the fingers do the work rather than lifting your whole hand.

The thumb generally plucks the bottom strings with downstrokes on the left side of the thumb and thumbnail. The other fingers pluck the higher strings using upstrokes with the fleshy tip of the fingers and fingernails. The thumb and fingers should pluck one string per stroke and not brush over several strings.

Another picking option you may choose to use is called hybrid picking (a.k.a. plectrum-style fingerpicking). Here, the pick is usually held between the thumb and first finger, and the three remaining fingers are assigned to pluck the higher strings.

THE LEFT HAND

The left-hand fingers are numbered 1 through 4.

Be sure to keep your fingers arched, with each joint bent; if they flatten out across the strings, they will deaden the sound when you fingerpick. As a general rule, let the strings ring as long as possible when playing fingerstyle.

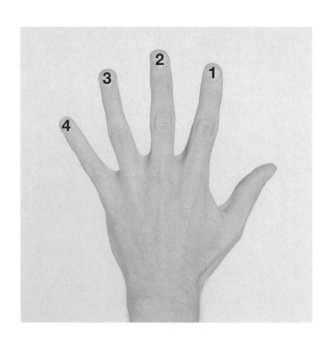

All of Me

Words and Music by John Stephens and Toby Gad

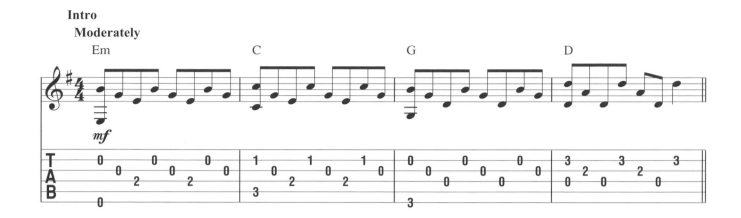

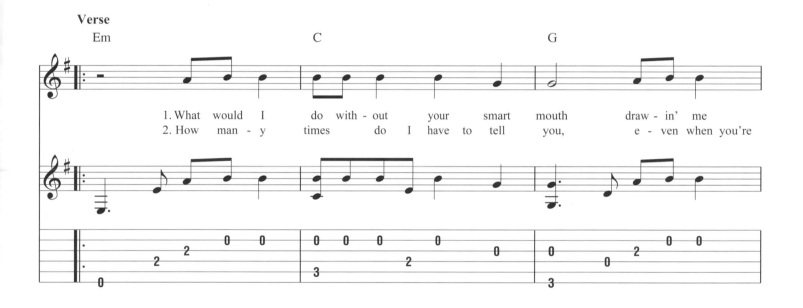

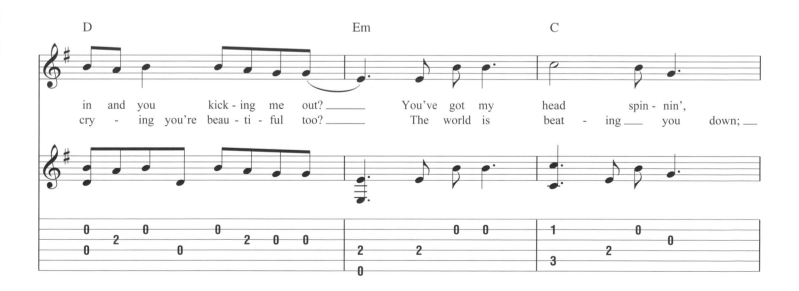

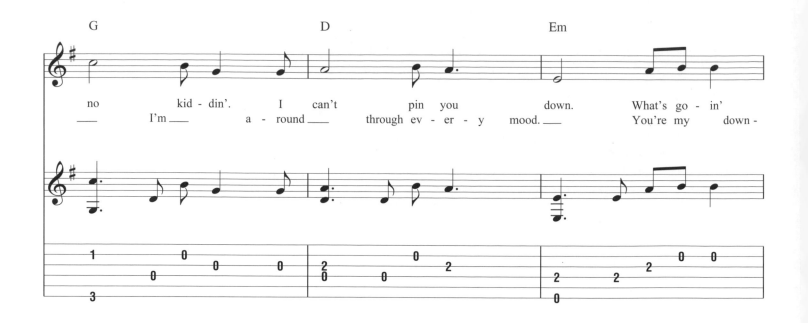

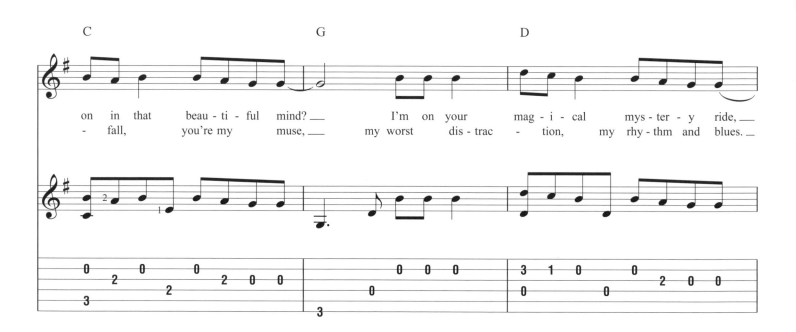

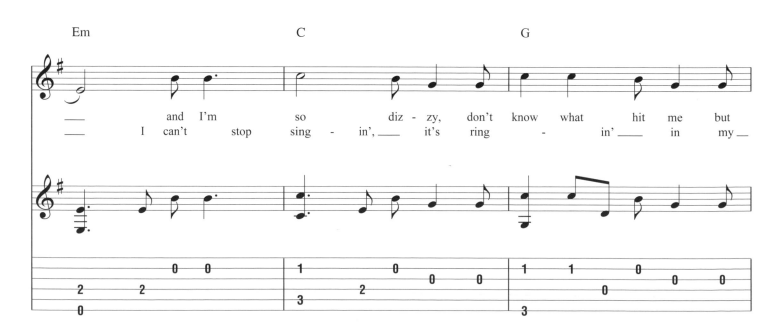

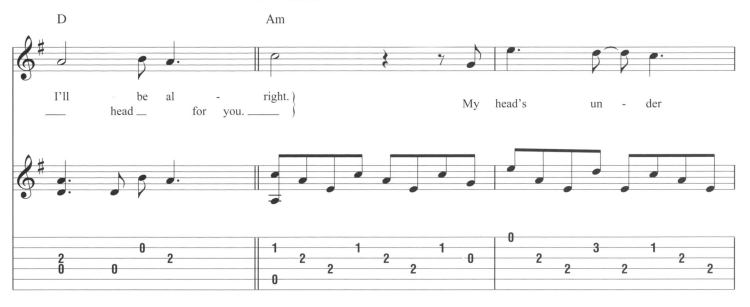

I'll   be   al   -   right.)   My   head's   un   -   der
__ head __ for you. ____)

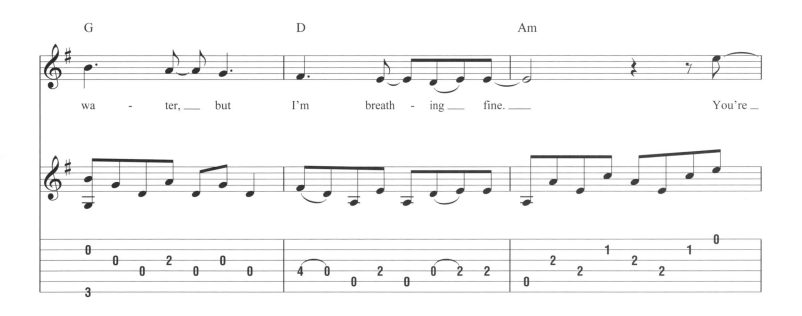

wa   -   ter, __ but   I'm   breath   -   ing __ fine. ____   You're __

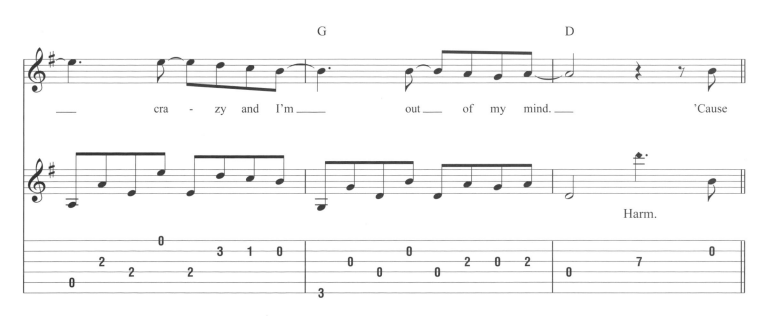

__ cra   -   zy and I'm ____ out __ of my mind. ____   'Cause

Harm.

𝄋 Chorus

all of me ___ loves all of you. ___ Love your

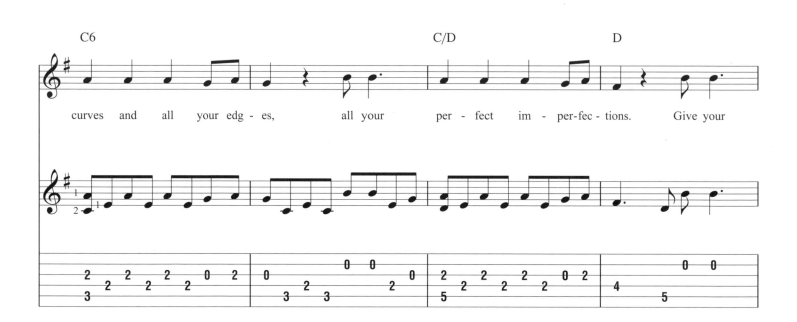

curves and all your edg — es, all your per - fect im - per-fec - tions. Give your

all to me, ___ I'll give my all to you. ___ You're my

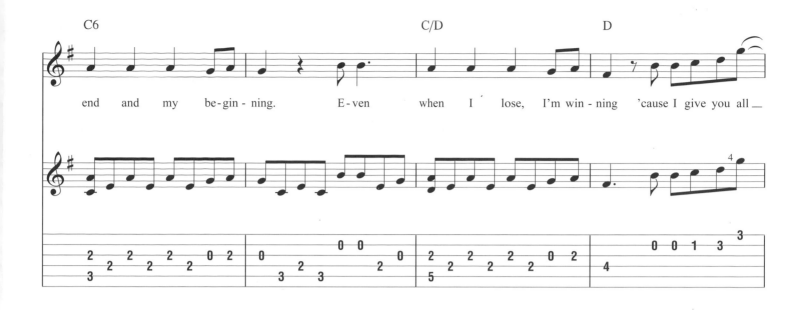

end and my be-gin - ning. E-ven when I lose, I'm win - ning 'cause I give you all __

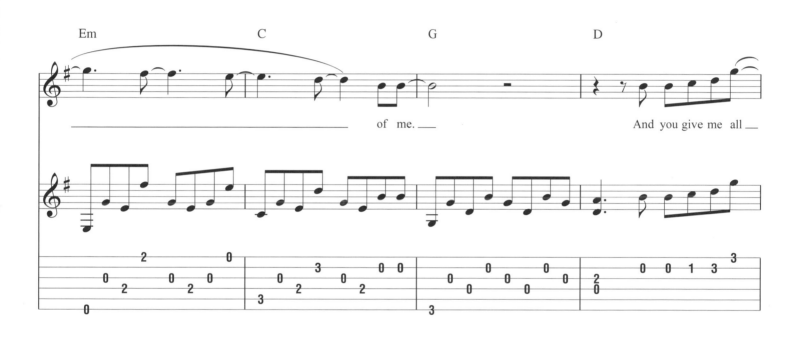

_____ of me. __ And you give me all __

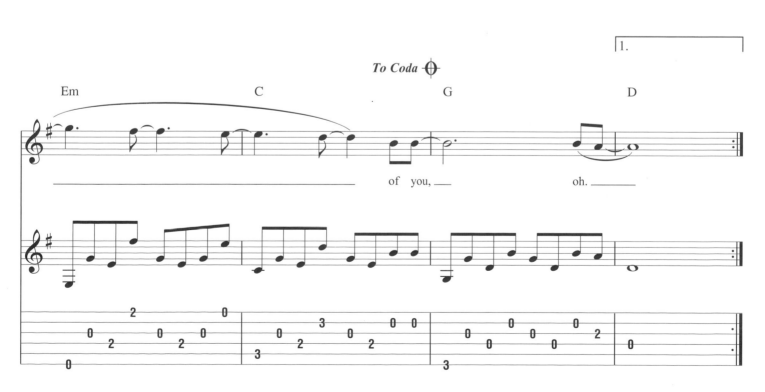

_____ of you, __ oh. _____

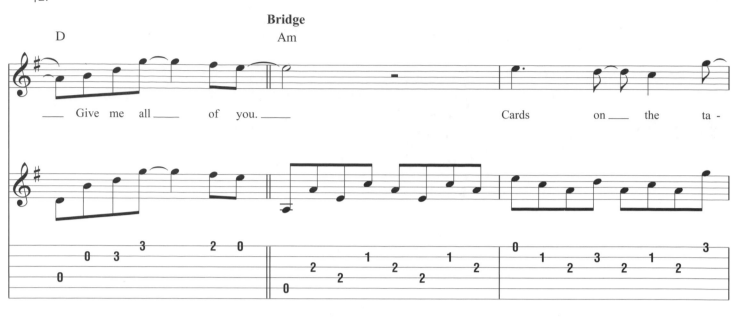

Give me all ___ of you. ___ Cards on ___ the ta-

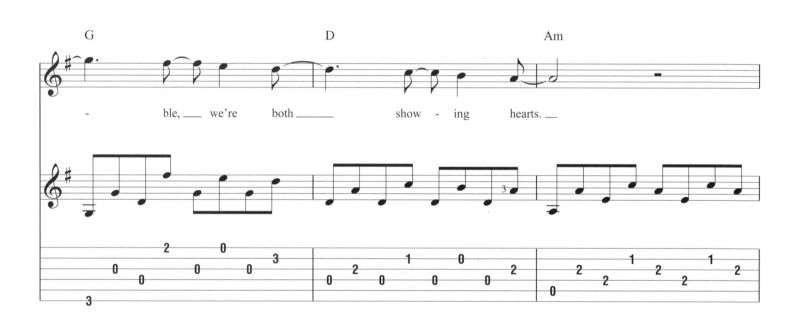

- ble, ___ we're both ___ show - ing hearts. ___

D.S. al Coda

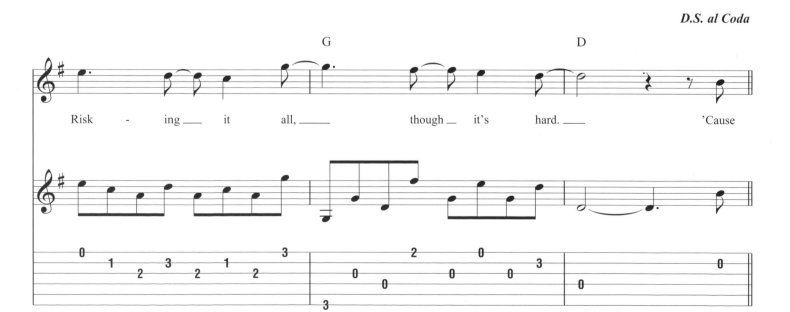

Risk - ing ___ it all, ___ though ___ it's hard. ___ 'Cause

⊕ Coda

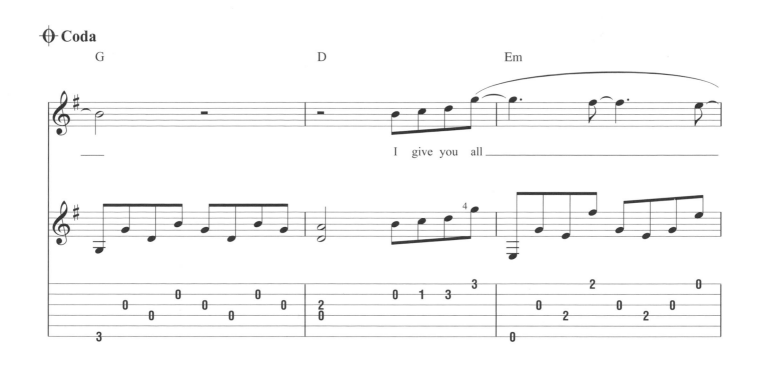

I give you all ___

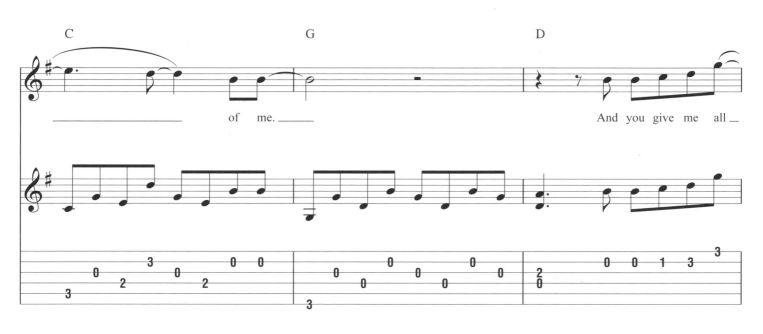

of me. ___ And you give me all ___

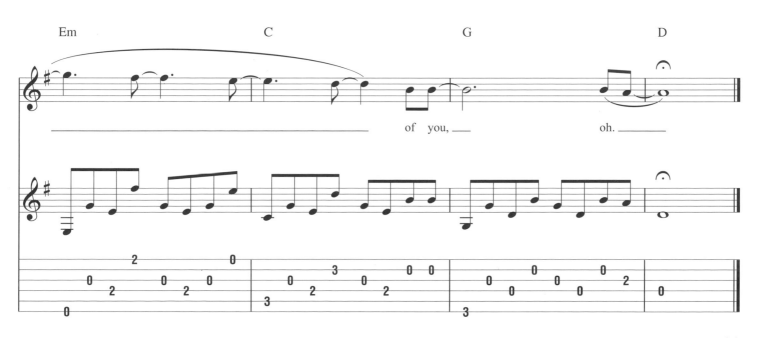

of you, ___ oh. ___

Brave

Words and Music by Sara Bareilles and Jack Antonoff

Verse
Moderately slow

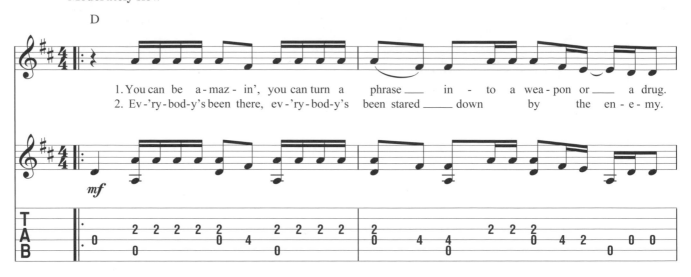

1. You can be a-maz-in', you can turn a phrase in-to a wea-pon or a drug.
2. Ev-'ry-bod-y's been there, ev-'ry-bod-y's been stared down by the en-e-my.

You can be the out-cast or be the back-lash of some-bod-y's lack of love,
Fall-en for the fear and done some dis-ap-pear-in' bow down to the might-y.

*Hold down 6th string
while lifting barre.

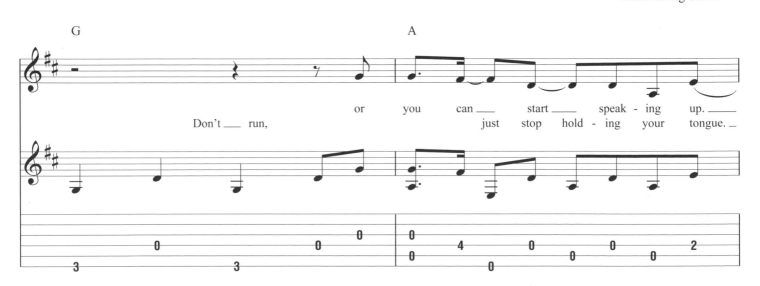

or you can start speak-ing up.
Don't run, just stop hold-ing your tongue.

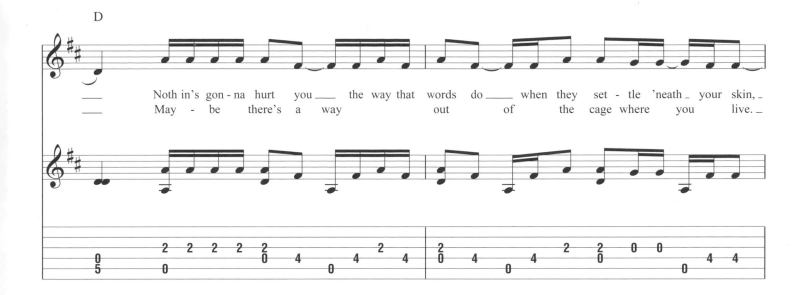

Noth in's gon - na hurt you ___ the way that words do ___ when they set - tle 'neath ___ your skin, ___
May - be there's a way ___ out of the cage where you live. ___

___ kept on the in - side ___ and no sun - light. Some - times a shad - ow
___ May - be one of these days you can let the light

*As before

wins. But I won - der what would hap - pen if you
in and show ___ me how big your brave is.

Chorus

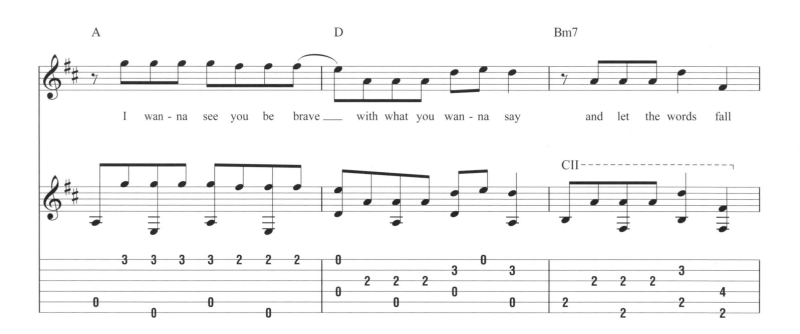

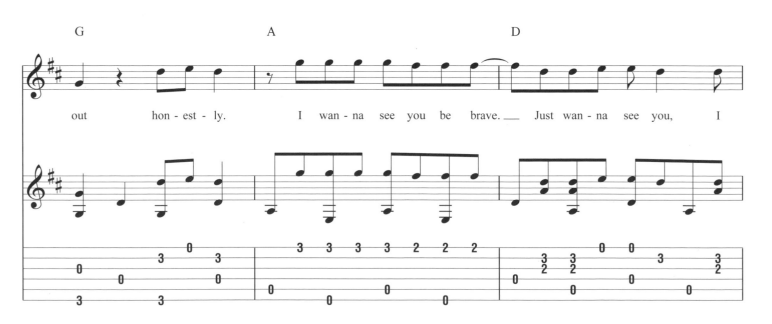

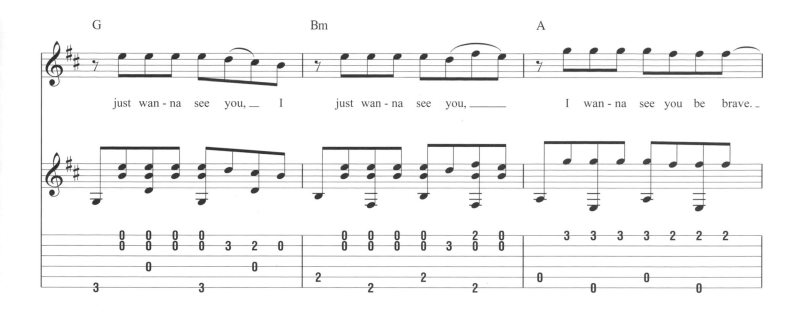

just wan-na see you, __ I just wan-na see you, _____ I wan-na see you be brave. __

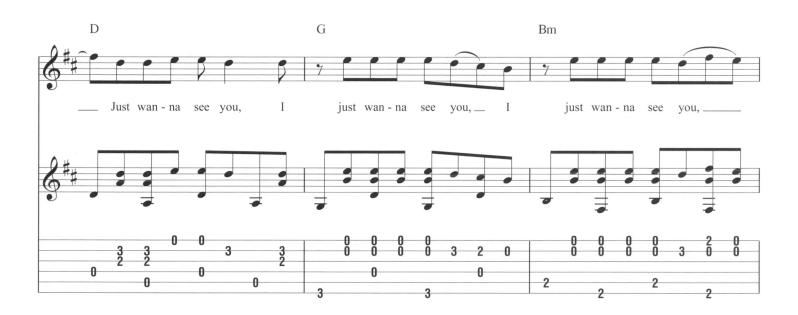

__ Just wan-na see you, I just wan-na see you, __ I just wan-na see you, _____

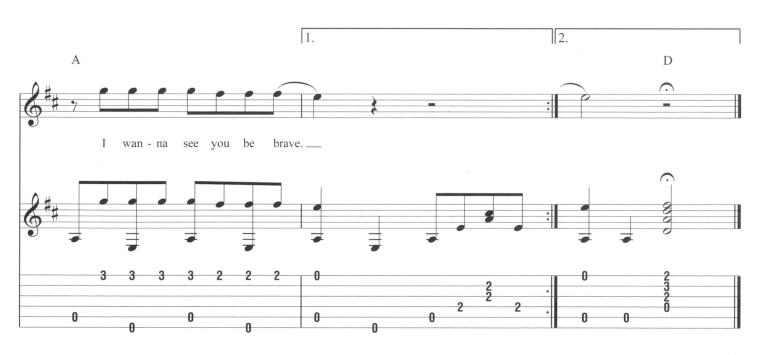

I wan-na see you be brave. __

Happy

from DESPICABLE ME 2
Words and Music by Pharrell Williams

1. It might seem cra - zy what I'm 'bout to say.
2. Here come bad news ___ talk - in' this and that.

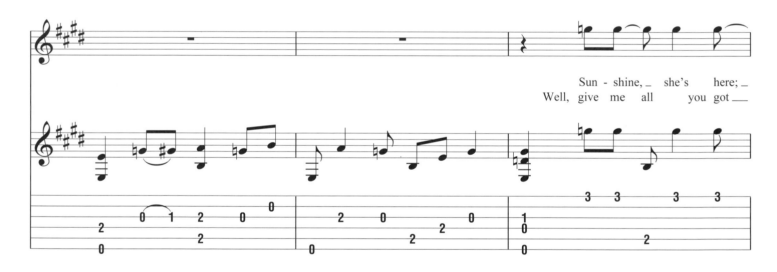

Sun - shine, ___ she's here; ___
Well, give me all you got ___

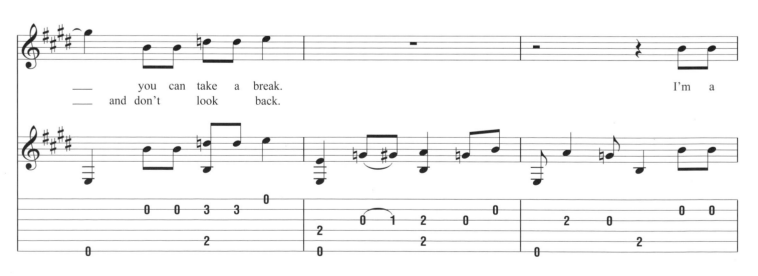

___ you can take a break. I'm a
___ and don't look back.

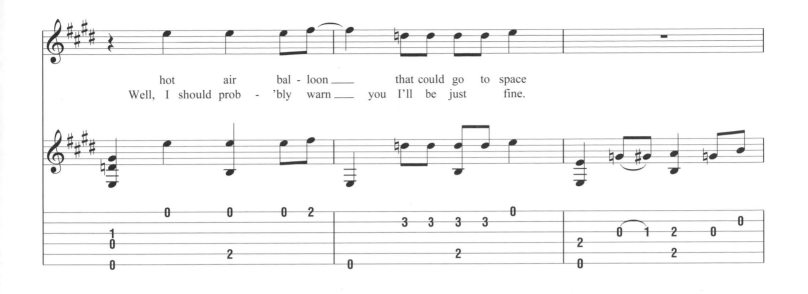

hot   air   bal - loon _____   that could go   to space
Well, I should prob - 'bly warn _____ you I'll be just   fine.

with   the   air _____   like   I   don't   care, _____
                              No of - fense   to   you _____

Bm

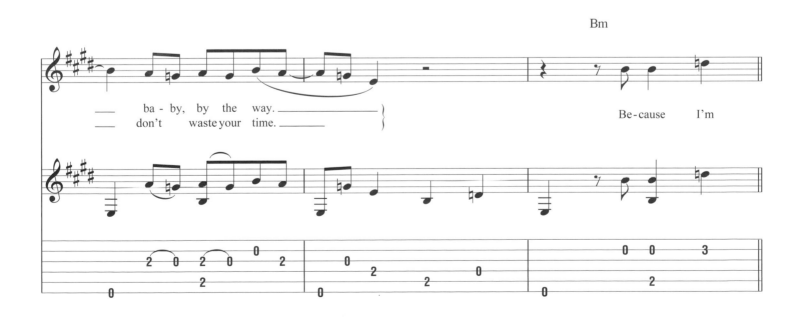

_____ ba - by, by the way. _____
_____ don't waste your time. _____

Be - cause   I'm

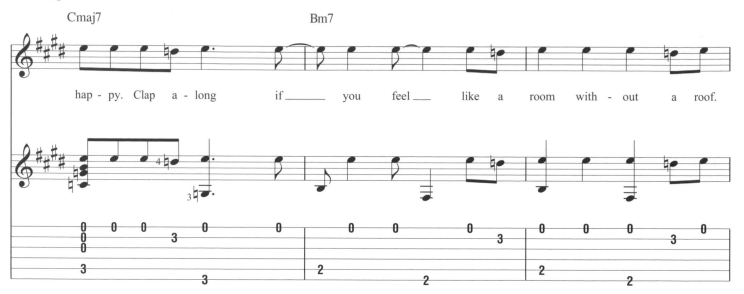

hap - py. Clap a - long   if ____ you   feel ____ like   a   room   with - out   a   roof.

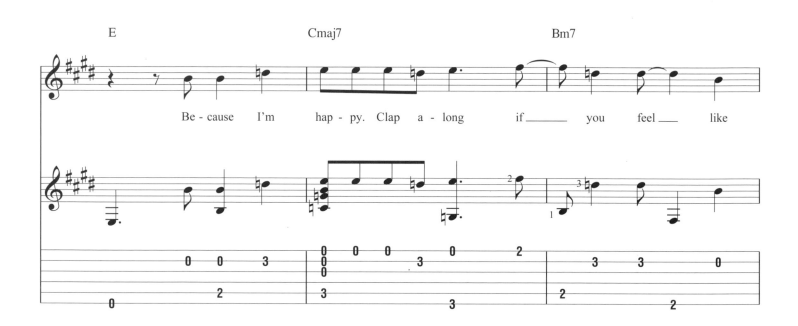

Be - cause   I'm   hap - py. Clap   a - long   if ____ you   feel ____ like

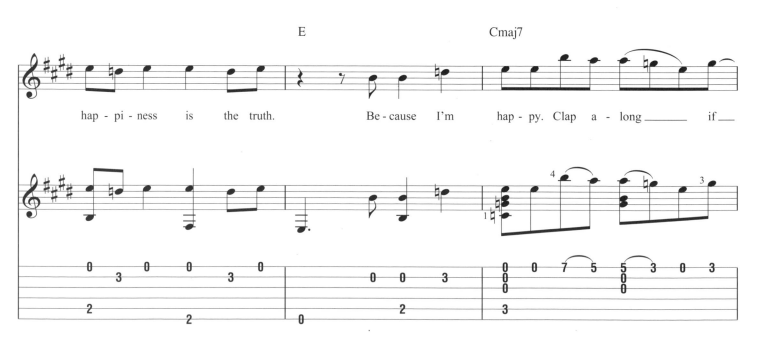

hap - pi - ness   is   the   truth.   Be - cause   I'm   hap - py. Clap   a - long ____ if ____

you know what hap-pi-ness is to you. Be-cause I'm hap-py. Clap a-long if _

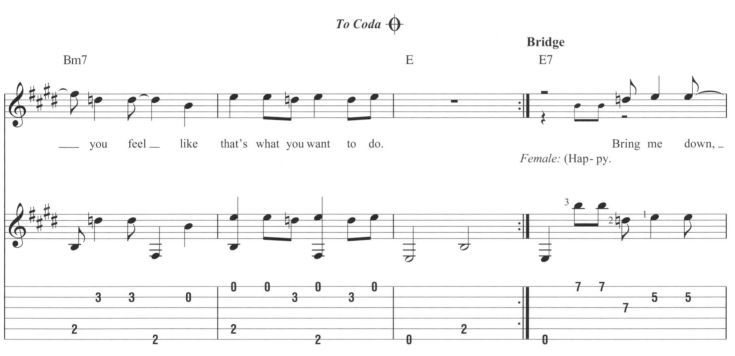

To Coda

Bridge

_you feel _ like that's what you want to do. Bring me down, _

Female: (Hap-py.

can't noth-in' bring me down; your love is too high. Bring me down, _
Hap-py. Hap-py.

19

can't noth - in'   bring me down. ___ Let me tell you now.
                                                      Hap - py.

                  Bring me   down, ___   can't noth - in'   bring me   down; _
Hap - py,   hap - py,   hap - py,   hap - py.   Hap - py,   hap - py,

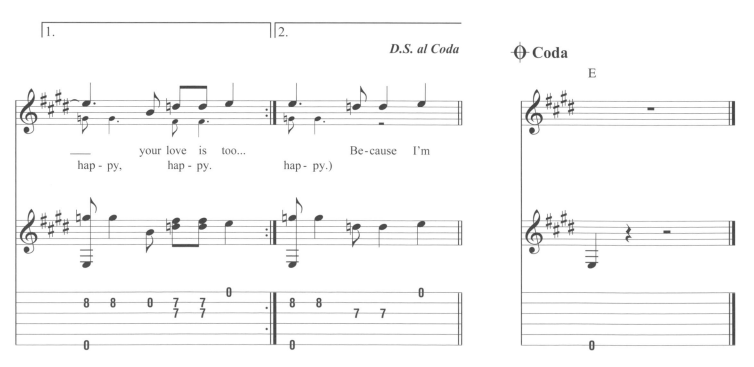

D.S. al Coda

Coda

E

___   your love is   too...   Be - cause I'm
hap - py,   hap - py.   hap - py.)

20

Ho Hey

Words and Music by Jeremy Fraites and Wesley Schultz

Intro

Moderately slow

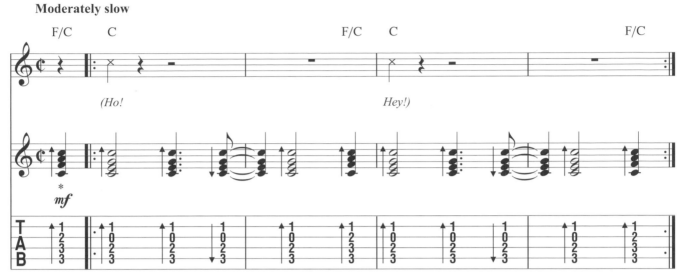

*Strum chords w/ index finger or thumb.

Verse

1. *(Ho!)* I've been try'n' to do ____ it right; *(Hey!)* I've been liv-in' a lone - ly life. ____

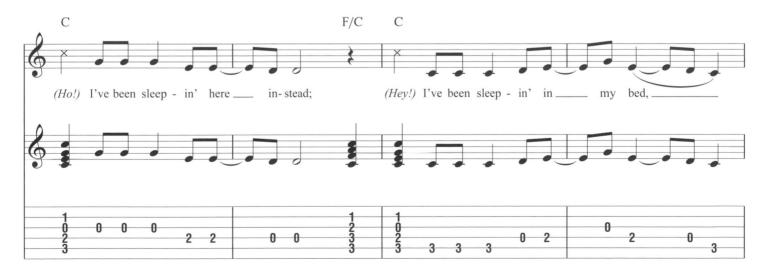

(Ho!) I've been sleep - in' here ____ in- stead; *(Hey!)* I've been sleep - in' in ____ my bed, ____

(Ho!) I've been sleep - in' in ____ my bed. ____ (Hey!

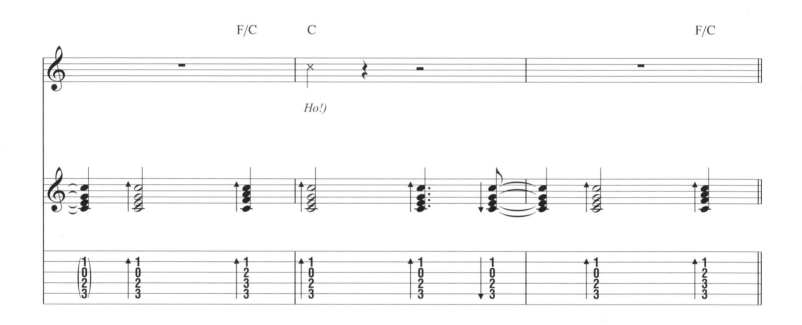

Ho!)

% Verse

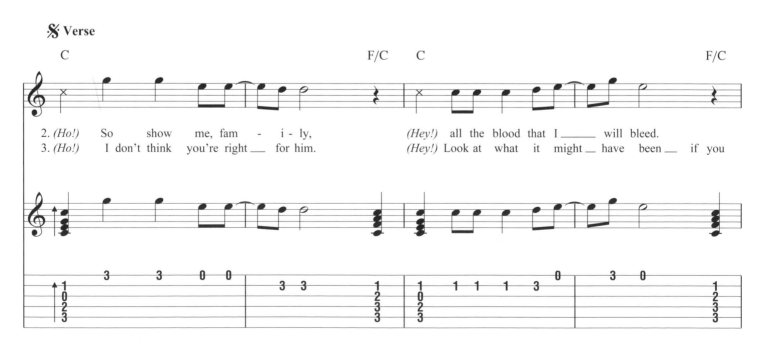

2. (Ho!) So show me, fam - i - ly,   (Hey!) all the blood that I ____ will bleed.

3. (Ho!) I don't think you're right ___ for him.   (Hey!) Look at what it might ___ have been ___ if you

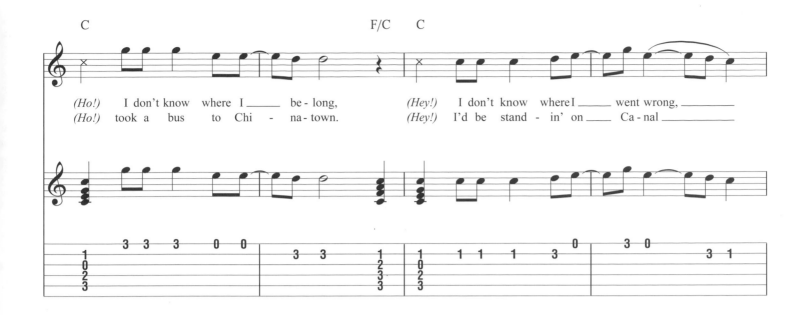

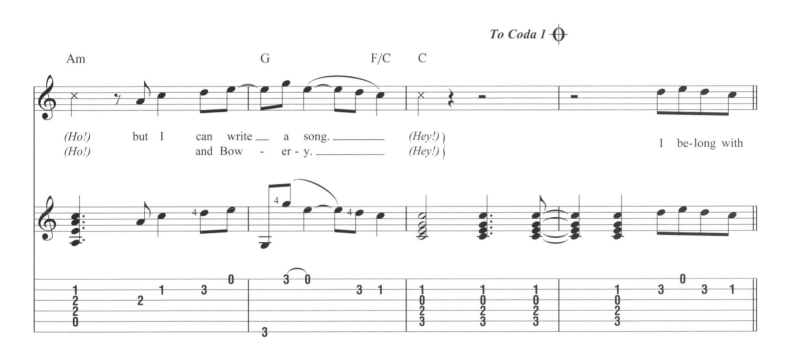

you, you be-long with me; you're my ___ sweet - heart.
(Ho!

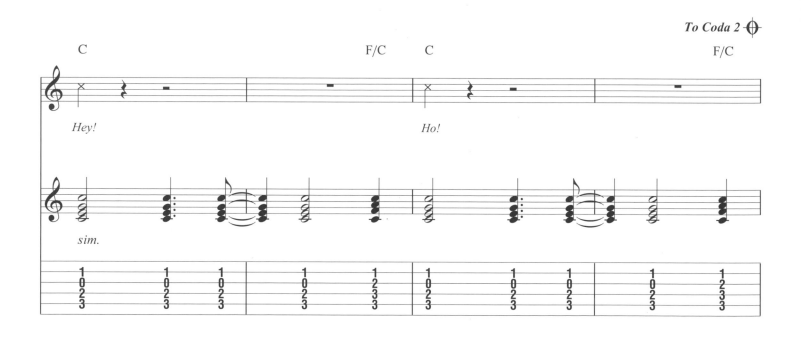

Hey!   Ho!

sim.

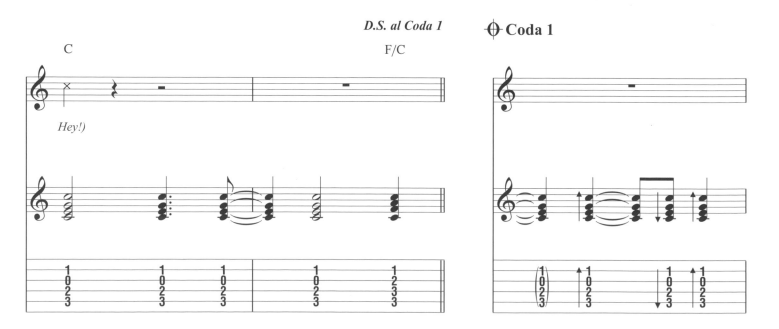

Hey!)

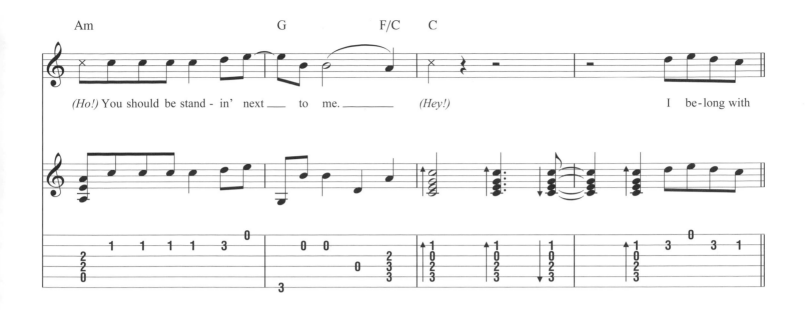

(Ho!) You should be stand - in' next ___ to me. _____ *(Hey!)*   I be-long with

Chorus

you,   you be - long with me;   you're my ___ sweet - heart. ___

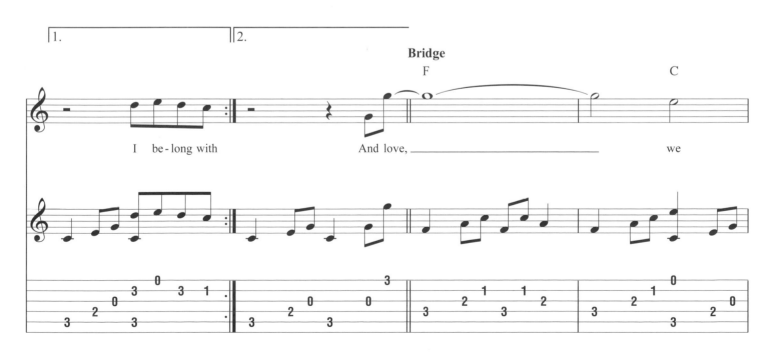

I be - long with   And love, _____ we

need   it   now. _____   Let's   hope, _____   for   some, _____

_____   'cause oh, _____   we're

D.S.S. al Coda 2   **⊕ Coda 2**

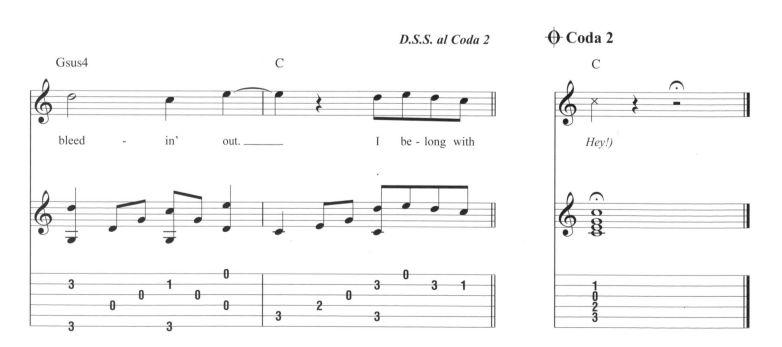

bleed - in'   out. _____   I be - long with   *Hey!)*

26

I Will Wait

Words and Music by Mumford & Sons

Intro
Moderately fast

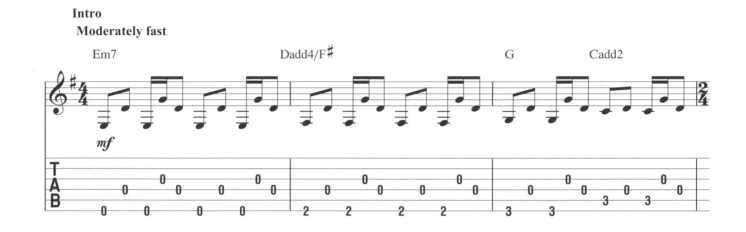

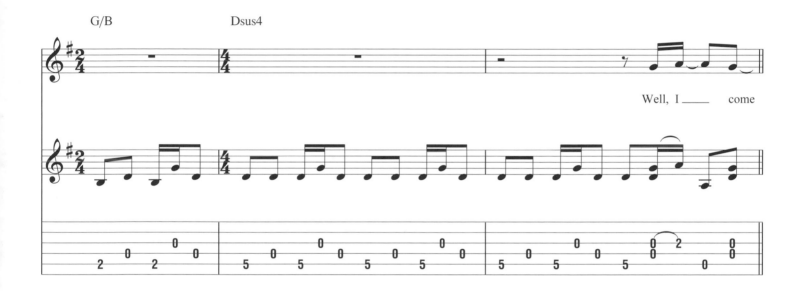

Well, I _____ come

Verse

_____ home _____
_____ step

like a _____ stone, _____
and re - lent. _____

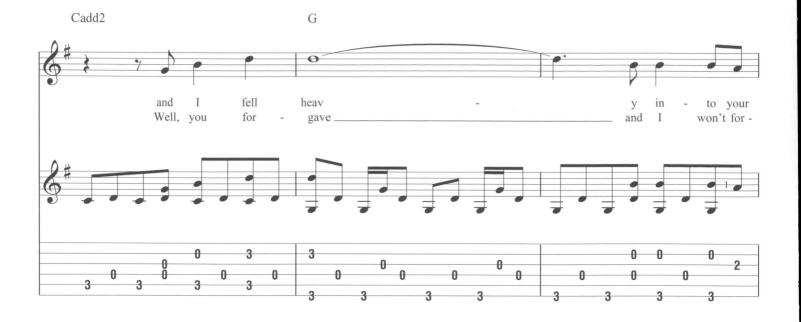

and I fell heav - y in - to your
Well, you for - gave and I won't for -

arms.
get.

These days of dust,
Know what we've seen,

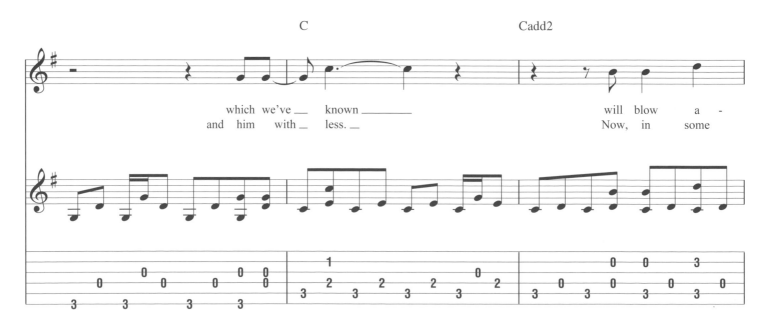

which we've known
and him with less.

will blow a -
Now, in some

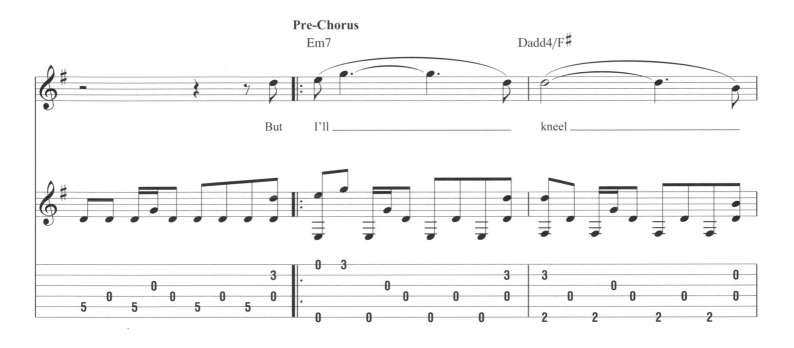

2nd time, To Coda ⊕

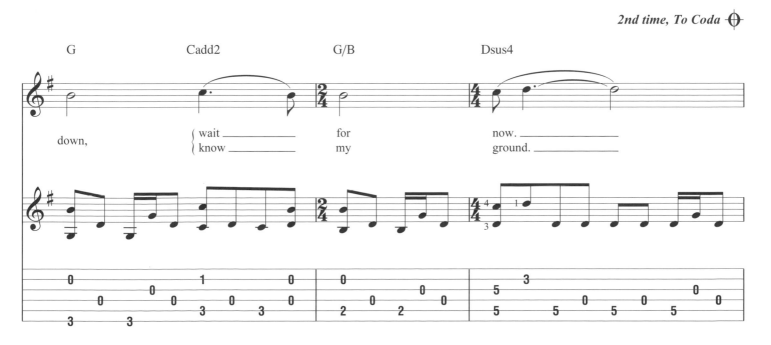

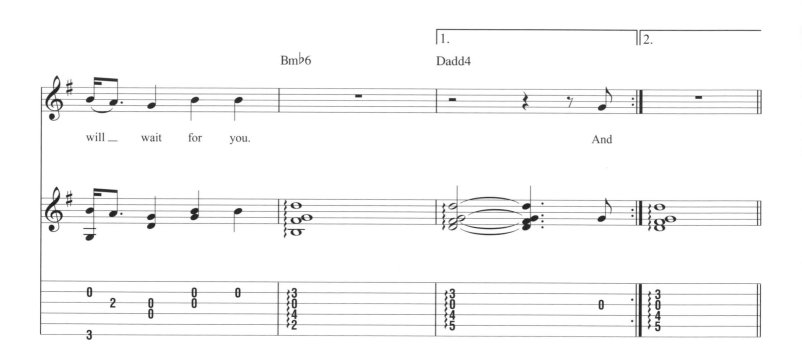

Interlude

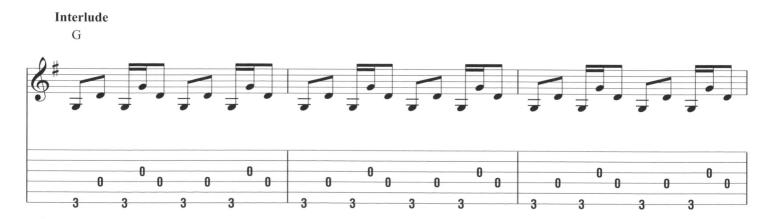

31

Jar of Hearts

Words and Music by Barrett Yeretsian, Christina Perri and Drew Lawrence

Pre-Chorus

I learned to live half a - live, and now you want me one more time.

Chorus

And who do you think you are, run - ning 'round leav - ing scars,

col - lect - ing your jar of hearts and tear - ing love a - part?

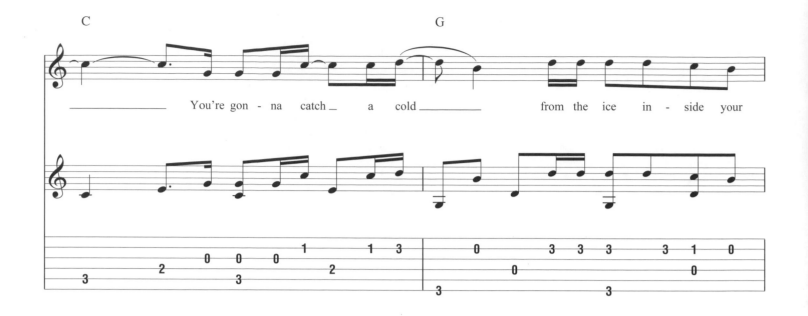

You're gon - na catch — a cold ____ from the ice in - side your

soul. ____ So don't come back — for me. Who do you think you are?

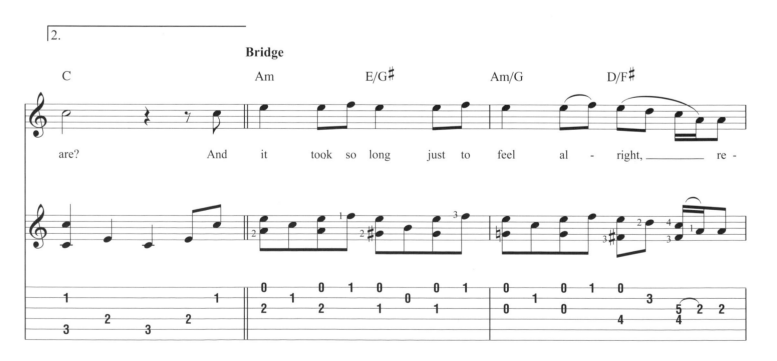

are? And it took so long just to feel al - right, ____ re -

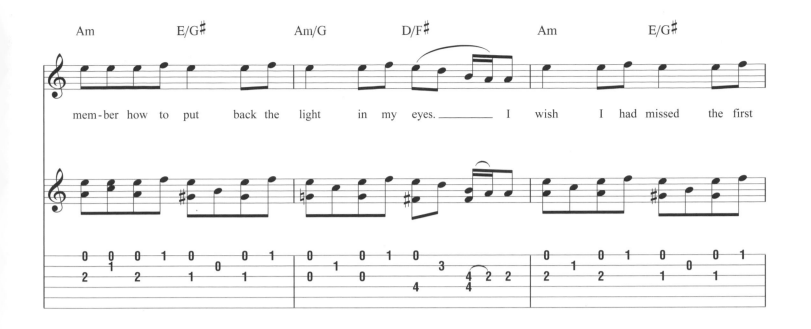

mem-ber how to put back the light in my eyes._____ I wish I had missed the first

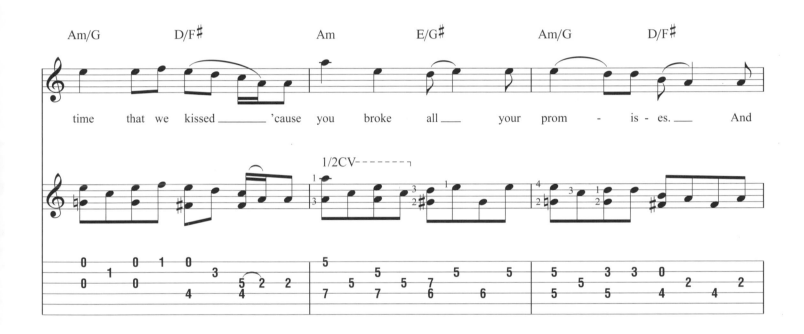

time that we kissed_____ 'cause you broke all ___ your prom - is - es. ___ And

now you're back, __ you don't get to get me back. _____

Chorus

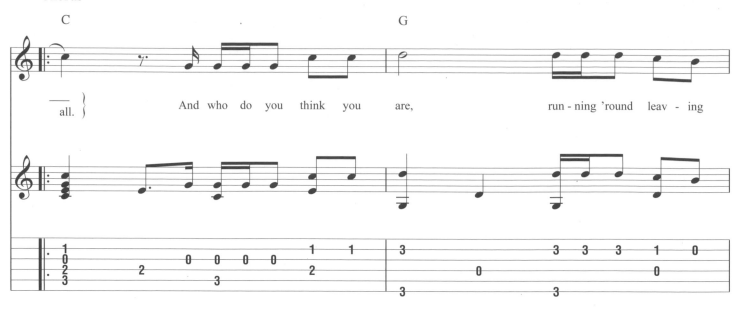

all.

And who do you think you are, run-ning 'round leav-ing

scars, _____ col - lect - ing your jar of hearts _____ and tear - ing love a - part? _

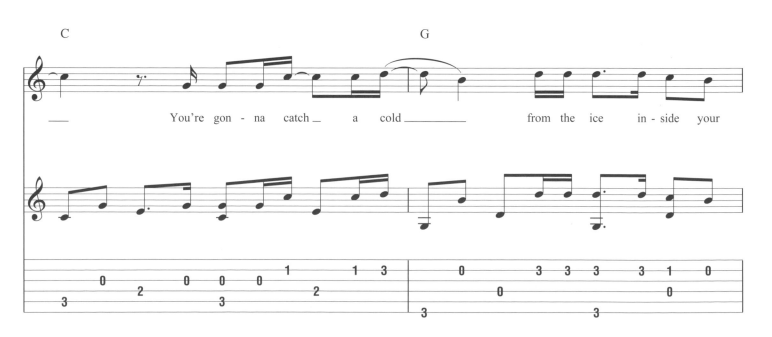

_ You're gon - na catch _ a cold _____ from the ice in - side your

So don't come back for me, don't come back at

Outro

all.   Who do you think you _____ are?

Who do you think you are?

Let It Go

from Disney's Animated Feature FROZEN
Music and Lyrics by Kristen Anderson-Lopez and Robert Lopez

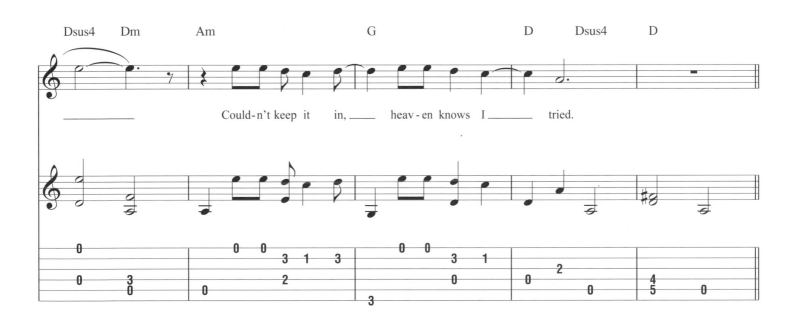

Pre-Chorus

Con-ceal, — don't feel, — don't let — them know... — Well, now —

𝄋 Chorus

— they know. _____ Let it go, ____
let it go; ____ can't
let it go; ____ I am one —

hold it back an-y - more. — Let it go, ____ let it go; _____ turn a - way —
— with the wind and sky. — Let it go, ____ let it go; _____ you'll nev -

and slam the door.
-er see me cry.

I don't care what they're
Here I stand, and

To Coda ⊕

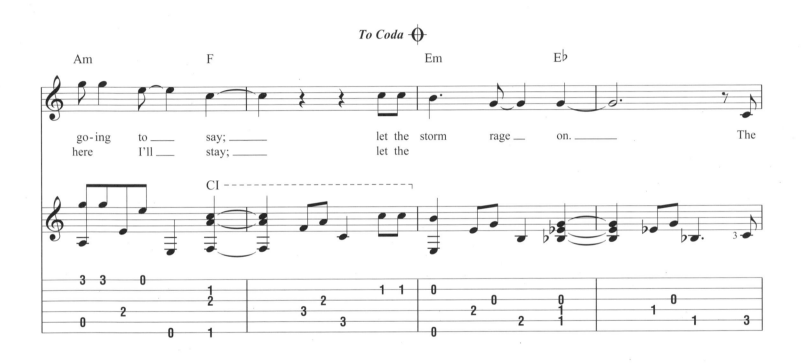

go-ing to say;
here I'll stay;

let the storm rage on. The
let the

cold nev-er both-ered me an-y-way.

Verse

2. It's fun-ny how some dis - tance makes ev - 'ry - thing _ seem   small; _   and the

fears that once _ con - trolled _ me   can't   get   to   me _ at   all. _

Pre-Chorus

It's time _ to   see ____ what I ____ can   do, ____   to test _ the lim - its   and _ break through. _

No right,— no wrong,— no rules— for me,——————— I'm free!————

D.S. al Coda

⊕ **Coda**

Let it go—

storm rage— on.———

The cold nev-er both-ered me an - y - way.————

Radioactive

Words and Music by Daniel Reynolds, Benjamin McKee, Daniel Sermon, Alexander Grant and Josh Mosser

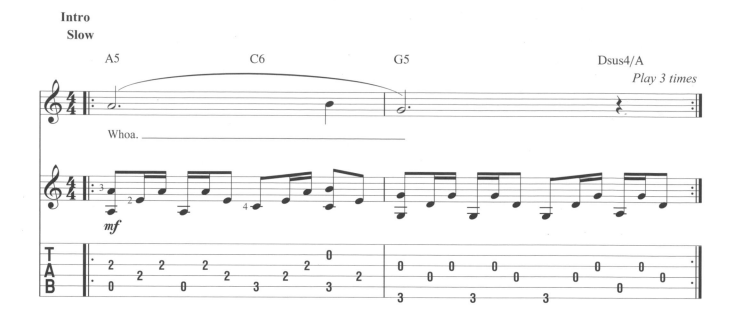

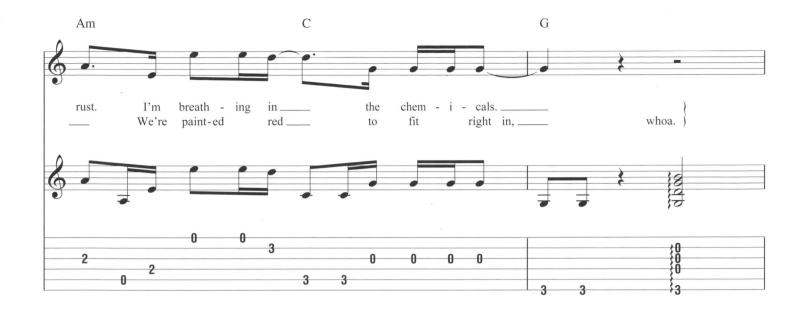

rust. I'm breath - ing in _____ the chem - i - cals. _____
_____ We're paint-ed red _____ to fit right in, _____ whoa.

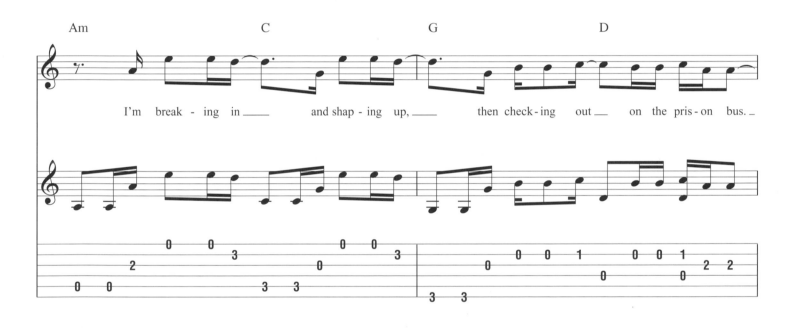

I'm break - ing in _____ and shap - ing up, _____ then check-ing out _____ on the pris - on bus. _____

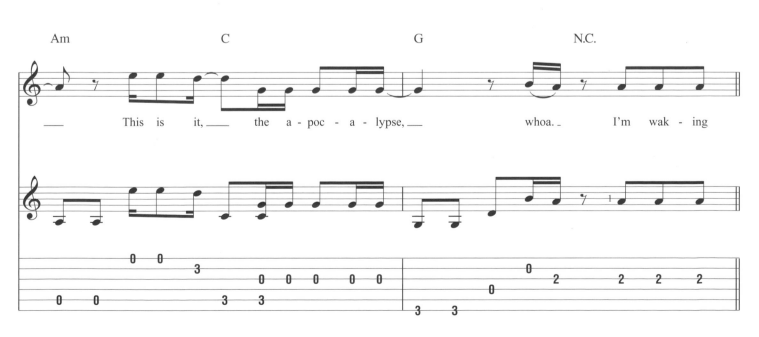

_____ This is it, _____ the a - poc - a - lypse, _____ whoa. _____ I'm wak - ing

Pre-Chorus

Chorus

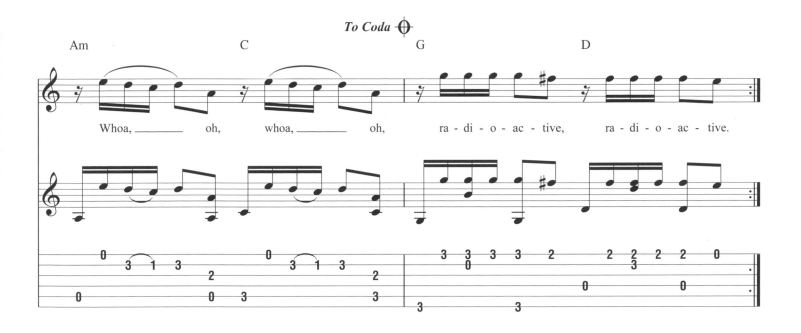

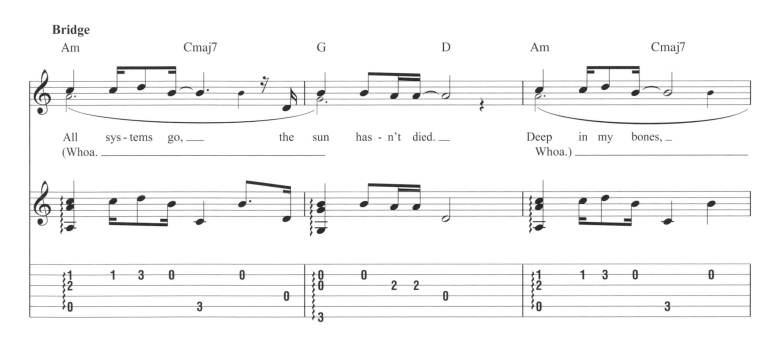

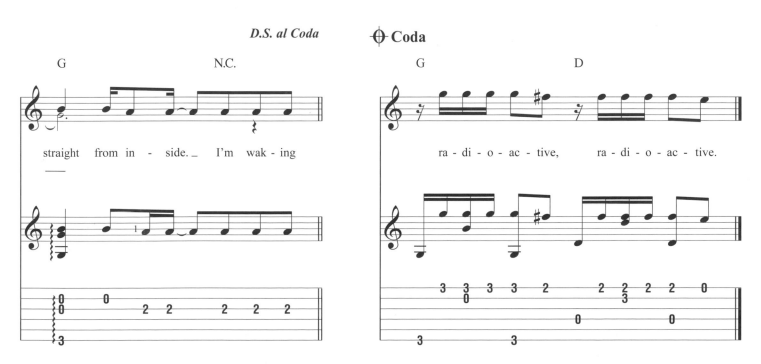

Royals

Words and Music by Ella Yelich-O'Connor and Joel Little

Drop D tuning:
(low to high) D-A-D-G-B-E

Intro

Moderately slow

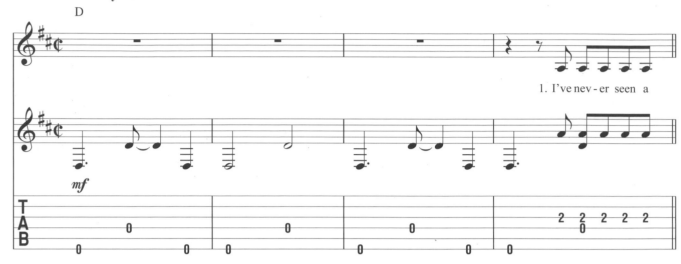

1. I've nev-er seen a

Verse

dia - mond in the flesh. ___
I, we've cracked the code. ___

I cut my
We count our

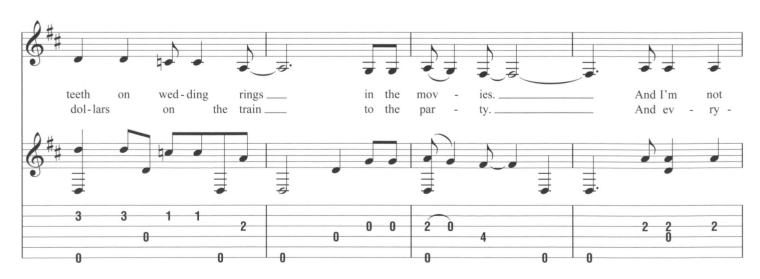

teeth on wed-ding rings ___ in the mov - ies. ___ And I'm not
dol-lars on the train ___ to the par - ty. ___ And ev - ry -

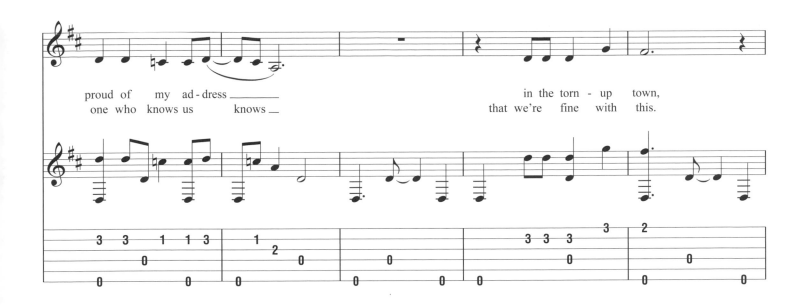

proud of my ad-dress _____ in the torn - up town,
one who knows us knows _____ that we're fine with this.

Pre-Chorus

D

no post - code en - vy. ——
We did-n't come from mon - ey. ——

But ev -'ry song's _ like { gold teeth, Grey Goose,
{ Cris - tal, May - bach,

C

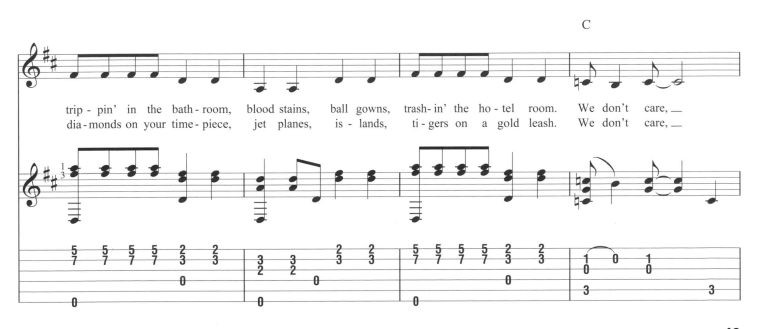

trip - pin' in the bath - room, blood stains, ball gowns, trash - in' the ho - tel room. We don't care, __
dia - monds on your time - piece, jet planes, is - lands, ti - gers on a gold leash. We don't care, __

Chorus

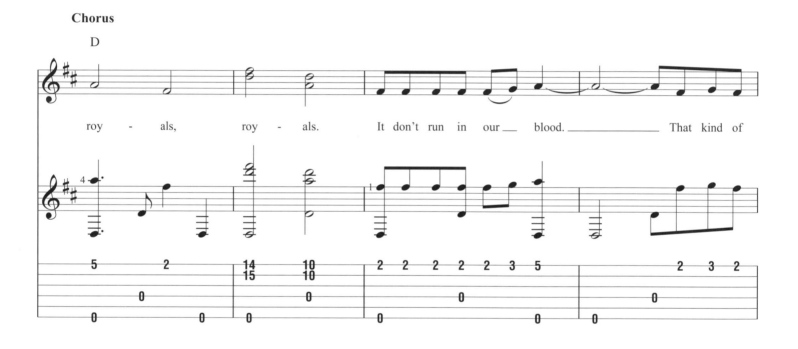

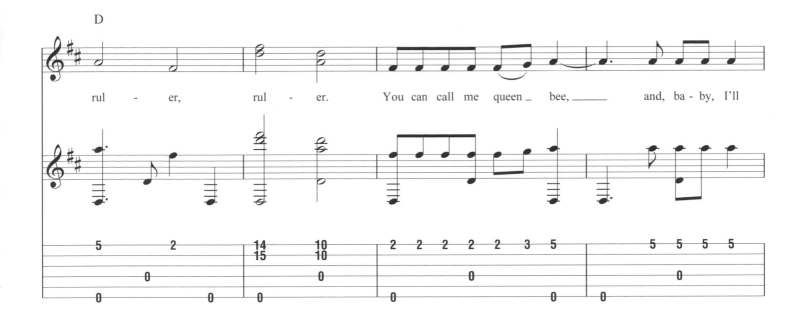

rul - er, rul - er. You can call me queen bee, and, ba - by, I'll

To Coda ⊕

Interlude

rule, I'll rule, I'll rule, I'll rule. Let me live that fan - ta - sy.

D.S. al Coda
(take repeat)

⊕ **Coda**

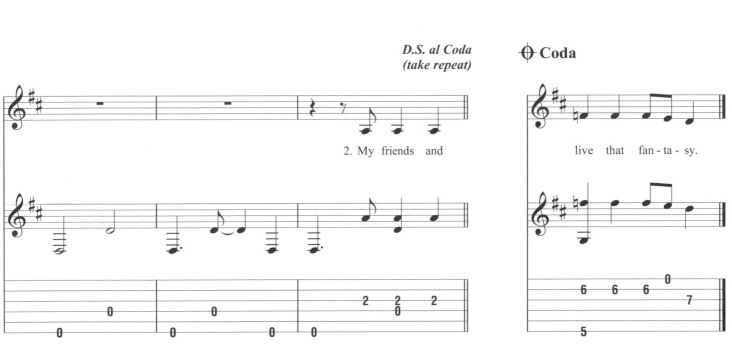

2. My friends and

live that fan - ta - sy.

Say Something

Words and Music by Ian Axel, Chad Vaccarino and Mike Campbell

Intro

Slow

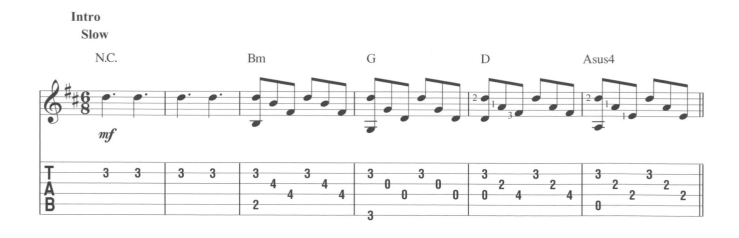

Chorus

Say some-thing, I'm giv-ing up on you.

I'll be the one if you want me to.

An-y-where   I   would have fol-lowed you.

Say some-thing,   I'm giv-ing   up   on you.

1. And

𝄋 Verse

I | am feel-ing so ___ small. | It was
I | will stum-ble and ___ fall. | I'm still
I | will swal-low my ___ pride. | You're the

G   D

o - ver my head; ___   I know noth - ing at ___ all.
learn - ing to love, ___   just start - ing to crawl.
one that I love, ___   and I'm say - ing good - bye.

Chorus

Asus4   Asus4   Bm   G

2. And   Say some-thing, I'm giv-ing up on you.

D   Asus4   Bm

I'm sor - ry that I ___

could - n't   get ___ to   you. ___

An - y - where   I   would have fol - lowed   you. _
And an - y - where

To Coda ⊕

Say some - thing, I'm giv - ing   up   on   you.

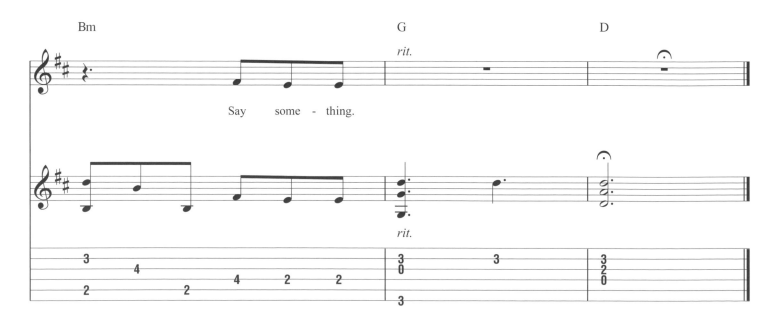

Skyfall

from the Motion Picture SKYFALL
Words and Music by Adele Adkins and Paul Epworth

count _____ to ten. ___   Feel   the ___ earth

move   and   then _____   hear   my ___ heart

burst   a - gain.   2. For   this

Verse

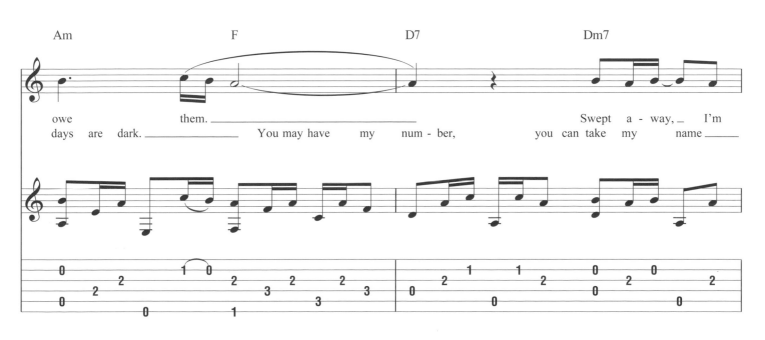

59

stol - but you'll nev - er have my heart. Let the

Chorus

sky fall. When it crum - bles, we will stand tall, face it

all to - geth - er. Let the sky fall. When it crum - bles, we will

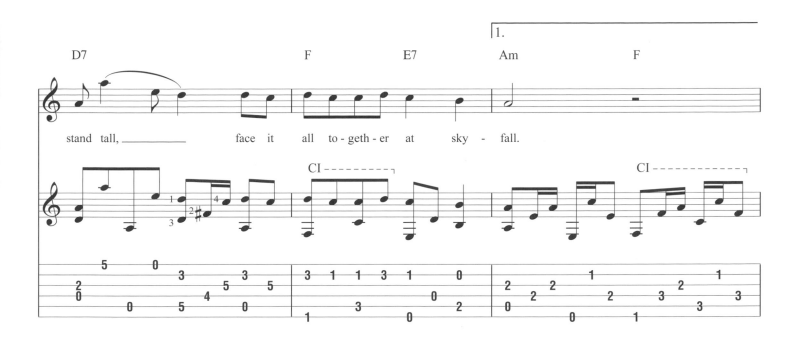

stand tall, _____ face it all to - geth - er at sky - fall.

At sky - fall.   3. Sky - fall is

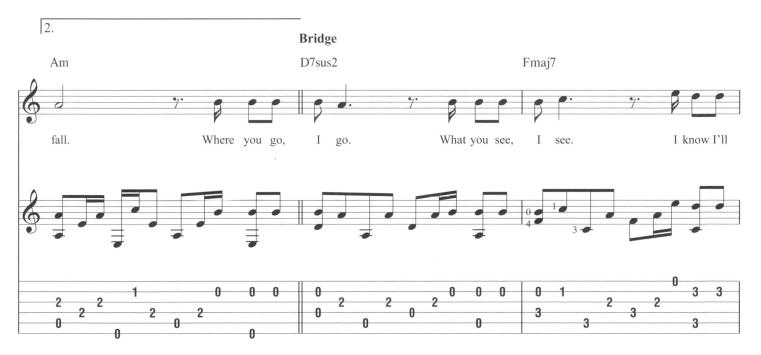

Bridge

fall.   Where you go,   I go.   What you see,   I see.   I know I'll

never be me ___ with-out the se - cu - ri - ty ___ of your lov-ing arms ___ keep-ing

D.S. al Coda
(take 1st ending)

me from harm. ___ Put your hand ___ in my hand ___ and we'll stand. ___ Let the

🅔 **Coda**

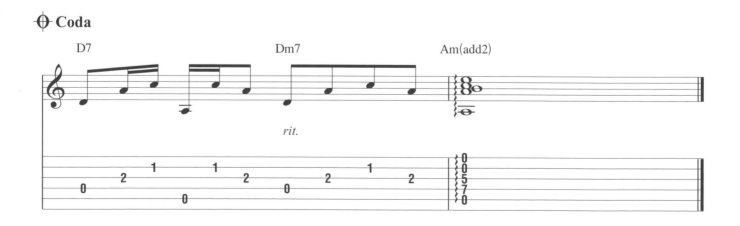

rit.

Stay

Words and Music by Mikky Ekko and Justin Parker

Intro
Moderately

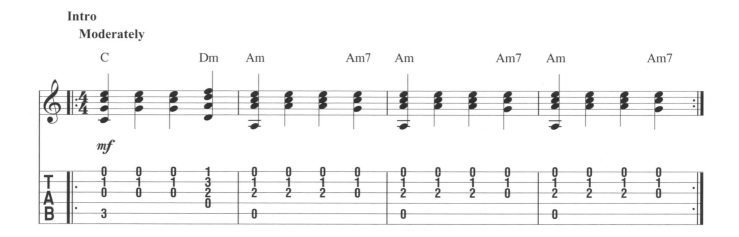

Verse

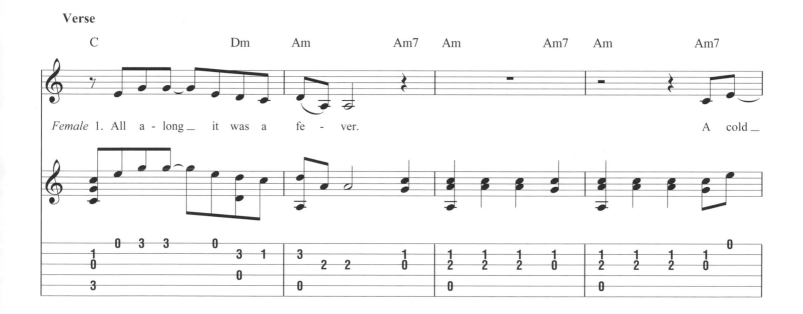

Female 1. All a-long __ it was a fe-ver. A cold __

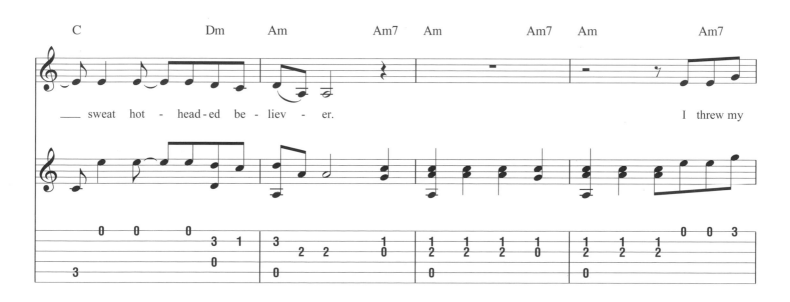

__ sweat hot-head-ed be-liev-er. I threw my

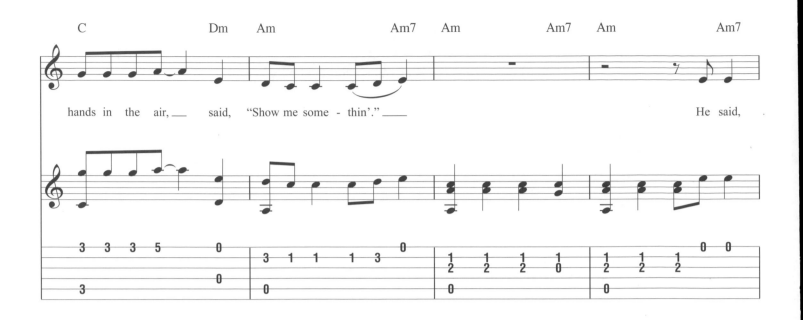

hands in the air, ___ said, "Show me some - thin'." ___ He said,

"If you dare, ___ come a lit - tle clos - er."

𝄋 Pre-Chorus

'Round and a-round and a-round and a-round we go. ___ Oh, ___

now, tell me now, tell me now, tell me now, tell me now you know. __

⅍⅍ Chorus

Not real-ly sure how to feel a-bout __ it. Some - thin' in the way you move __ makes __

To Coda 2 ⊕

__ me feel like I can't __ live with-out __ you. {Well,}/{Yeah,} it __ takes me all the way. __ I want you to stay. __

To Coda 1

Male: 2. It's not much of a

life you're liv- in'.   It's not ___ just some - thin' you take; it's giv- en.

D.S. al Coda 1   ⊕ **Coda 1**

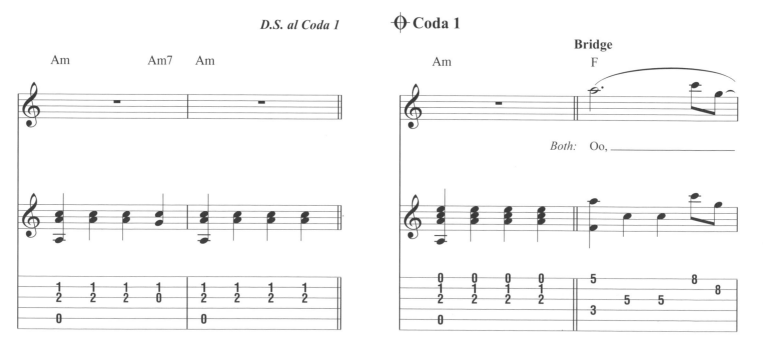

Both: Oo, _____

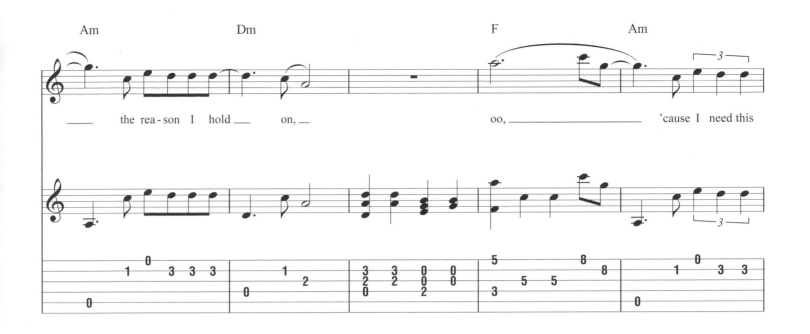

the rea-son I hold ___ on, ___ oo, _____ 'cause I need this

hole ___ gone. ___ Fun - ny you're the bro-ken one but I'm the on - ly one who need-ed

sav - in'. 'Cause when you nev - er see the light, it's hard to know which one of us is

D.S.S. al Coda 2

⊕ **Coda 2**

Outro

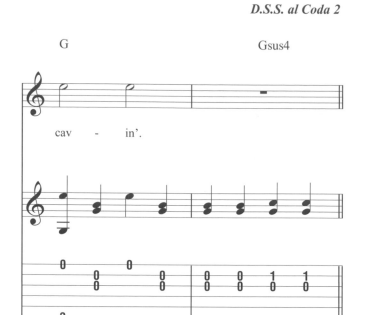

cav - in'.

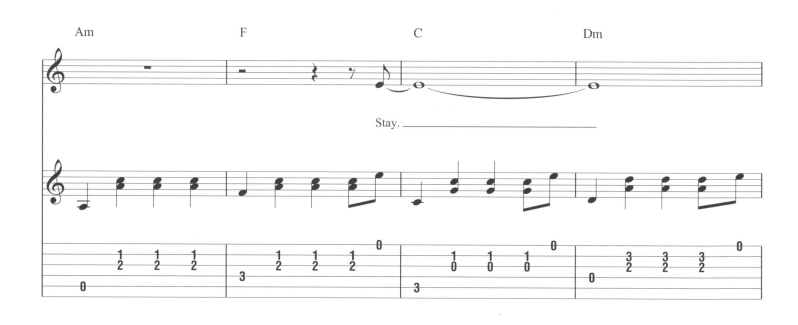

Stay. _____

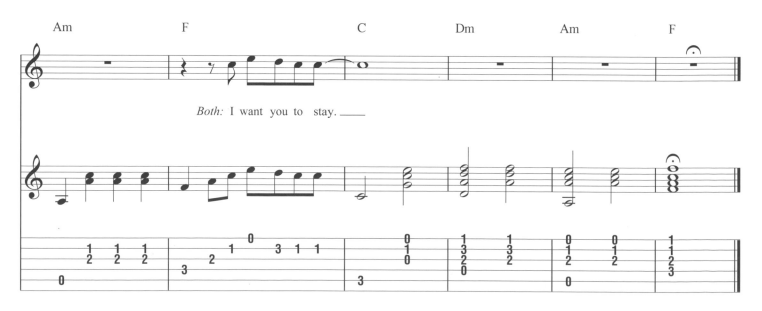

Both: I want you to stay. ____

Stay with Me

Words and Music by Sam Smith, James Napier and William Edward Phillips

These nights nev - er seem _ to go to plan.
And deep down I _____ know _ this nev - er works.

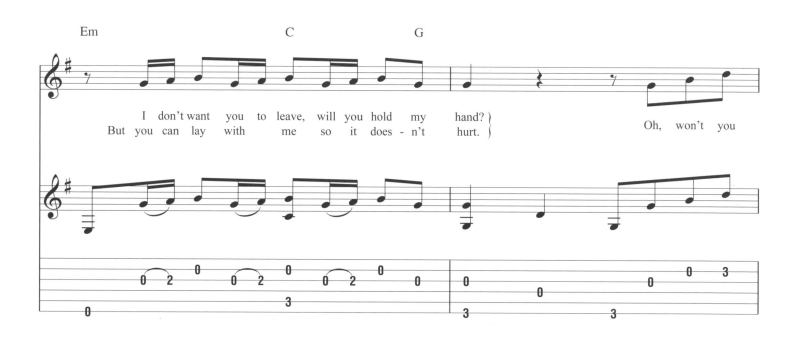

I don't want you to leave, will you hold my hand?
But you can lay with me so it does - n't hurt.

Oh, won't you

% Chorus

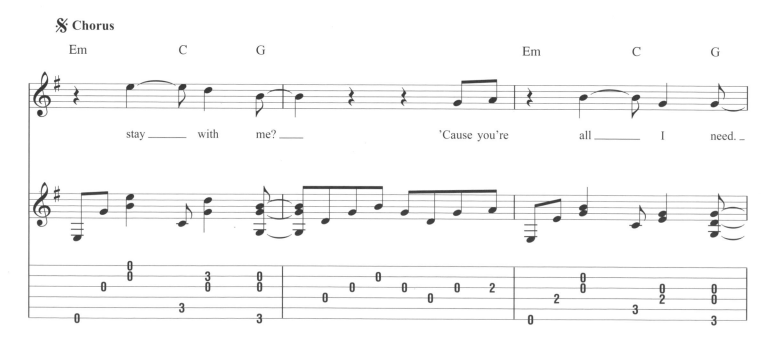

stay _____ with me? _____ 'Cause you're all _____ I need. _

70

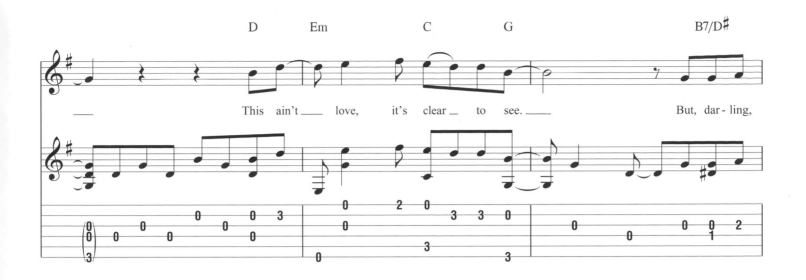

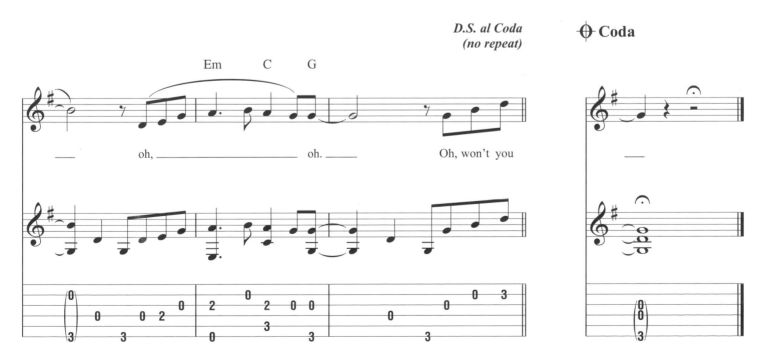

When I Was Your Man

Words and Music by Bruno Mars, Ari Levine, Philip Lawrence and Andrew Wyatt

Same bed, but it feels just a lit-tle bit big-ger now.
My pride, my e-go, my needs and my self-ish ways

Our song on the ra-di-o, but it don't sound the same.
caused a good strong wom-an like you to walk out my life.

Now, I'll

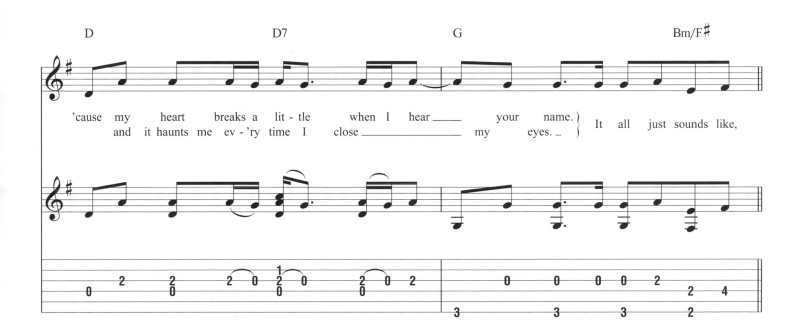

Pre-Chorus

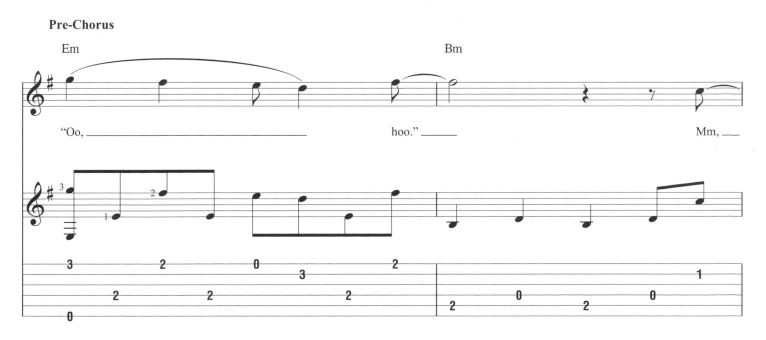

too young, too dumb to re - al - ize _____ that I should-'ve bought you flow-

$ Chorus

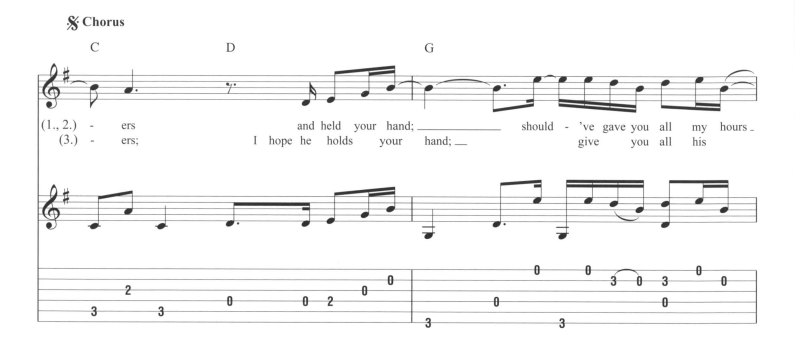

(1., 2.) - ers and held your hand; _____ should - 've gave you all my hours _
(3.) - ers; I hope he holds your hand; _ give you all his

_____ when I had the chance; _____ take _ you to ev - 'ry par -
hours _ when he has the chance; take you to ev-'ry par -

- ty, 'cause all ___ you want - ed to do ___ was dance. ___ Now, ___ my ba - by's danc -
- ty, ___ 'cause I re - mem - ber how much ___ you love to dance; ___ do ___ all the things I ___

1.

- ing, ___ but she's danc - ing with an - oth - er man. ___

2.

— Al - though it

Bridge

hurts, I'll be the first _____ to say _____ that _____ I was

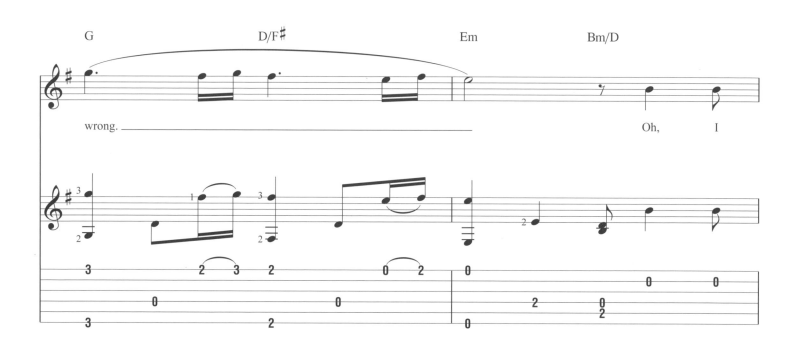

wrong. _____ Oh, I

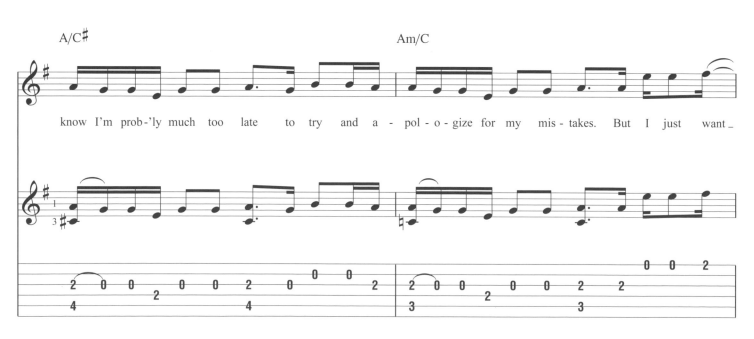

know I'm prob-'ly much too late to try and a - pol - o - gize for my mis - takes. But I just want _

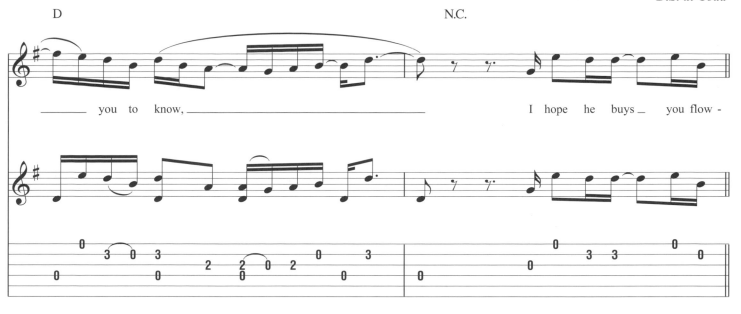

you to know, _____ I hope he buys___ you flow -

Coda

___ should-'ve done when I was your man._____ Do ___ all the things I ____

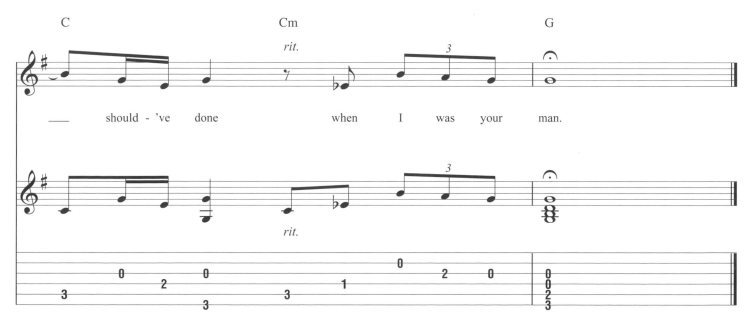

___ should - 've done when I was your man.

FINGERPICKING GUITAR BOOKS

Hone your fingerpicking skills with these great songbooks featuring solo guitar arrangements in standard notation and tablature. The arrangements in these books are carefully written for intermediate-level guitarists. Each song combines melody and harmony in one superb guitar fingerpicking arrangement. Each book also includes an introduction to basic fingerstyle guitar.

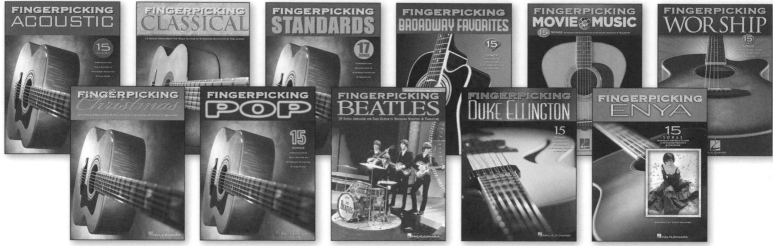

FINGERPICKING ACOUSTIC
00699614...$14.99

FINGERPICKING ACOUSTIC CLASSICS
00160211...$14.99

FINGERPICKING ACOUSTIC HITS
00160202...$12.99

FINGERPICKING ACOUSTIC ROCK
00699764...$12.99

FINGERPICKING BALLADS
00699717...$12.99

FINGERPICKING BEATLES
00699049...$19.99

FINGERPICKING BEETHOVEN
00702390...$8.99

FINGERPICKING BLUES
00701277 ....$9.99

FINGERPICKING BROADWAY FAVORITES
00699843...$9.99

FINGERPICKING BROADWAY HITS
00699838...$7.99

FINGERPICKING CELTIC FOLK
00701148...$10.99

FINGERPICKING CHILDREN'S SONGS
00699712...$9.99

FINGERPICKING CHRISTIAN
00701076 ....$7.99

FINGERPICKING CHRISTMAS
00699599...$9.99

FINGERPICKING CHRISTMAS CLASSICS
00701695...$7.99

FINGERPICKING CHRISTMAS SONGS
00171333...$9.99

FINGERPICKING CLASSICAL
00699620...$10.99

FINGERPICKING COUNTRY
00699687...$10.99

FINGERPICKING DISNEY
00699711...$15.99

FINGERPICKING EARLY JAZZ STANDARDS
00276565 ....$12.99

FINGERPICKING DUKE ELLINGTON
00699845...$9.99

FINGERPICKING ENYA
00701161...$10.99

FINGERPICKING FILM SCORE MUSIC
00160143...$12.99

FINGERPICKING GOSPEL
00701059...$9.99

FINGERPICKING GUITAR BIBLE
00691040 ....$19.99

FINGERPICKING HIT SONGS
00160195...$12.99

FINGERPICKING HYMNS
00699688...$9.99

FINGERPICKING IRISH SONGS
00701965...$9.99

FINGERPICKING ITALIAN SONGS
00159778...$12.99

FINGERPICKING JAZZ FAVORITES
00699844...$9.99

FINGERPICKING JAZZ STANDARDS
00699840...$10.99

FINGERPICKING ELTON JOHN
00237495...$12.99

FINGERPICKING LATIN FAVORITES
00699842...$9.99

FINGERPICKING LATIN STANDARDS
00699837...$12.99

FINGERPICKING ANDREW LLOYD WEBBER
00699839...$14.99

FINGERPICKING LOVE SONGS
00699841...$12.99

FINGERPICKING LOVE STANDARDS
00699836 ....$9.99

FINGERPICKING LULLABYES
00701276...$9.99

FINGERPICKING MOVIE MUSIC
00699919...$10.99

FINGERPICKING MOZART
00699794...$9.99

FINGERPICKING POP
00699615...$12.99

FINGERPICKING POPULAR HITS
00139079...$12.99

FINGERPICKING PRAISE
00699714...$10.99

FINGERPICKING ROCK
00699716...$12.99

FINGERPICKING STANDARDS
00699613...$12.99

FINGERPICKING WEDDING
00699637...$9.99

FINGERPICKING WORSHIP
00700554...$10.99

FINGERPICKING NEIL YOUNG – GREATEST HITS
00700134...$14.99

FINGERPICKING YULETIDE
00699654...$9.99

HAL•LEONARD®

Visit Hal Leonard online at **www.halleonard.com**

Prices, contents and availability
subject to change without notice.

0619
279

AUTHENTIC CHORDS • ORIGINAL KEYS • COMPLETE SONGS

The *Strum It* series lets players strum the chords and sing along with their favorite hits. Each song has been selected because it can be played with regular open chords, barre chords, or other moveable chord types. Guitarists can simply play the rhythm, or play and sing along through the entire song. All songs are shown in their original keys complete with chords, strum patterns, melody and lyrics. Wherever possible, the chord voicings from the recorded versions are notated.

THE BEACH BOYS' GREATEST HITS
00699357.............................. $12.95

THE BEATLES FAVORITES
00699249.............................$15.99

VERY BEST OF JOHNNY CASH
00699514.............................$14.99

CELTIC GUITAR SONGBOOK
00699265.............................$12.99

CHRISTMAS SONGS FOR GUITAR
00699247.............................$10.95

CHRISTMAS SONGS WITH 3 CHORDS
00699487.............................$9.99

VERY BEST OF ERIC CLAPTON
00699560.............................$12.95

JIM CROCE – CLASSIC HITS
00699269.............................$10.95

DISNEY FAVORITES
00699171.............................$14.99

MELISSA ETHERIDGE GREATEST HITS
00699518.............................$12.99

FAVORITE SONGS WITH 3 CHORDS
00699112.............................$10.99

FAVORITE SONGS WITH 4 CHORDS
00699270.............................$8.95

FIRESIDE SING-ALONG
00699273.............................$12.99

FOLK FAVORITES
00699517.............................$8.95

THE GUITAR STRUMMERS' ROCK SONGBOOK
00701678.............................$14.99

BEST OF WOODY GUTHRIE
00699496.............................$12.95

JOHN HIATT COLLECTION
00699398.............................$17.99

THE VERY BEST OF BOB MARLEY
00699524.............................$14.99

A MERRY CHRISTMAS SONGBOOK
00699211.............................$10.99

MORE FAVORITE SONGS WITH 3 CHORDS
00699532.............................$9.99

THE VERY BEST OF TOM PETTY
00699336.............................$15.99

BEST OF GEORGE STRAIT
00699235.............................$16.99

TAYLOR SWIFT FOR ACOUSTIC GUITAR
00109717.............................$16.99

BEST OF HANK WILLIAMS JR.
00699224.............................$16.99

Visit Hal Leonard online at
www.halleonard.com

Prices, contents & availability subject to change without notice.

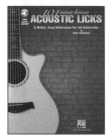